more to keep

us warm

more to keep us warm

Jacob Scheier

MISFIT

ECW Press

Published by ECW PRESS, 2120 Queen Street East, Suite 200,
Toronto, Ontario, Canada M4E 1E2

LIBRARY AND ARCHIVES CANADA CATALOGUING IN PUBLICATION

Scheier, Jacob
More to keep us warm / Jacob Scheier.

"a misFit book."
Poems.
ISBN 978-1-55022-794-9
1. Title.

PS8637.C432M67 2007   C811'.6   C2007-903574-4

Editor for the press: Michael Holmes / a misFit book
Type: Mary Bowness
Cover Art: Jason Kieffer
Cover Design: David Gee
Author Photo: Henry King
Production: Rachel Brooks
Second printing: Coach House Printing

The publication of *More to Keep Us Warm* has been generously supported by the
Canada Council for the Arts, which last year invested $20.1 million in writing and
publishing throughout Canada, by the Ontario Arts Council, by the Government of
Ontario through Ontario Book Publishing Tax Credit, and the Government
of Canada through the Book Publishing Industry Development Program (BPIDP).

 Canada Council   Conseil des Arts
for the Arts   du Canada   Canada    ONTARIO ARTS COUNCIL
CONSEIL DES ARTS DE L'ONTARIO

PRINTED AND BOUND IN CANADA

ECW PRESS
ecwpress.com

contents

II here,

poetry can't hurt you

III can it ever be
cancelled?

ACKNOWLEDGEMENTS

Thank you to Di Brandt and Robert Priest for their ongoing advice, support and feedback in the process of writing this book.

Thank you to everyone at ECW Press, especially Michael Holmes for his invaluable suggestions and guidance throughout the editing process.

Thank you to my family, in particular my father, Yossi Schwartz.

Thank you also to Phlip Arima, Clara Blackwood, Allan Briesmaster, Peter Bowen, Trang Cao, John Cook, Nashira Dernesch, Rocco de Giacomo, Pier Giorgio Di Cicco, Marty Gervais, Fran Harwood, Reverend Brent Hawkes, Meghan Hunter, Jet Fuel Coffee Shop, Jason Kieffer, Henry King, Monica S. Kuebler, Daniel Marrone, Chris Matthews, Rowan McNamara, Sarah Pinder, Paisley Rae, Dawna Rae Hicks, Yorgos Stamatopoulos, Richard Teleky, Priscila Uppal, Myna Wallin, Golnaz Zad and all my former classmates from the creative writing program at York University.

Thank you to my friends in the Toronto poetry community for their support and encouragement.

Thank you to the Ontario Arts Council for their financial support.

Thank you to *Descant* and *The White Wall Review*.

For my mother, Libby (Liebe) Scheier (1946–2000)
and Jim McNamara

"Love is not consolation, it is light."

    – Simone Weil

"I did not care what it was all about. All I wanted to know was how to live in it."

    – Ernest Hemingway

I

quickly approaching

the beginning

THE VOICES

It's alright for the rich and the healthy to keep still;
no one wants to know about them anyway.
But those in need have to step forward,
have to say: I am blind,
or, I am about to go blind,
or, nothing is going well with me,
or, I have a child who is sick,
or, right here I'm sort of glued together.

And probably that isn't enough.

They have to sing; if they didn't sing, everyone
would walk past, as if they were fences or trees.

That's where you hear the good singing.

People are strange: they prefer
to hear castratos in choirs.

But God himself comes and stays awhile
when the world of torn and cut people starts to humble him.

"The Voices" is a collaborative translation, with Di Brandt, of Rainer Maria Rilke's
"Title Poem for *The Voices*"

GENESIS

"The perceptual disturbances may include . . . trailing images
(images left suspended in the path of a moving object as seen
in stroboscopic photography), perceptions of entire objects,
afterimages (a same-colored or complementary-colored 'shadow'
of an object remaining after the removal of the object), halos
around objects . . ."

— Description of Hallucinogen Persisting
Perception Disorder, *DSM IV*

i. First there was the word
and I only had sounds.

First there was the word:
mother

taught me the names
of the fowl of the air
and every beast in the field,
and father

was no word for the absence
of mother,

my name,
lost somewhere inside her,
before it reached
her mouth, still (and) open.

2. In the beginning
of without
the word, I named again
the air and field
sounds clumped together
and lit the open mouth
in the face of the deep.

3. And it was good
enough.

4. But He said unto me:
it can always be better
and He had many letters after his name,
blessing him
with authority.

He cured,
not with touch or speech,
but something small and round
to swallow.

When I doubted,
when I said I can slither through it,
He spoke unto me: you do not know
what I know,
and held out the thin branch of his arm
and I followed,
I obeyed.

5. And on the seventh day
the earth collapsed.

On the seventh day
I lost part of my sight.

6. First there was the word
and it was blurred.

The shadow of each letter
ate into the next.

And darkness was upon the face of the deep.

7. The names (again) turned to absence.
I could not call this smeared yellow thing
a flower.
I could not name this thing,
encircled in a ghostly halo
and spraying light in a hundred directions,
the moon.

Without names,
I was not master of the animals,
but lost amongst monsters.

BIG BAND MUSIC

It is music which could only be written before the second war,
before the soundtrack of Europe was composed by mice
running along piano keys.
It is music meant for how our bodies used to be,
before the dance steps we learned
became a talent for avoiding the land mines beneath our feet.
There is something in the pace of the rhythm,
how it doesn't slow to take in a landscape,
how it assumes the world will still be there
when the music stops.

The song is replaced by the hourly news,
the wars which are now commercials between melodies.
I turn off the radio and lie still
taking in all the sounds my body makes
when all else is quiet.
How fragile and clumsy this machinery seems.

I am lying here waiting for an assassin
with the wrong address
or something heavy
like love or a piano
to fall on me.

I am surprised that just once
my heart hasn't forgotten (to beat)
like when I confuse the days of the week
or which people are still alive.
How my heart still remembers
to pump blood through my body
when I forget so easily

all the little things that need to be done
to remain alive:
to look both ways before crossing the street
and forgive people
before tumors fill their ears
and they can only hear decay.

I have been lying here so long
I can recognize the chorus of my breath.
And I think I have just been shot
when the phone rings.
This could be The Call.
The million dollar call,
the Jesus call,
Virginia Woolf explaining the day
she chose the heaviness of stones
and anonymity of rivers
over the weight and light of the world.

I have been lying here too long
to distinguish war from suicide.

HOW TO WRESTLE AN ANGEL

1. Wrestle him all night, till the breaking of dawn.
Fight dirty if necessary. Bite and pull his wings,
do not let him go until he blesses you.

2. Stand perfectly still.
Let his wings slap against your flesh all night.
Do not move or make a sound. Try to blink as little as possible,
even when a feather smacks hard into your balls,
even then do not scream.
Do not ask to be blessed.
Receive him in silence,
even if it kills you.

3. Make sarcastic, derogatory remarks about angels
each time he hits you.
Then say to him how much *Angels in America* pales
to *Doctor Faustus*.
Tell him "Even if you were God himself
I would not let you bless me"
and mean it.

4. Invite him into your home,
serve him wine and cheesecake
or beer and pork rinds, whatever is handy.
Play chess or Monopoly, Truth or Dare.
After a few glasses, talk of former lovers and parents.
After a few more, compliment his voice,
express admiration for his wing span,
then caress his spirit.
Let him fall asleep in your arms
and while he dreams
write *evil* on his forehead.

GENESIS OF FALLING OUT

How little is described in those pages.
We do not know which flowers grew
between the first man and woman,
which ones blossomed
like the offering of an open hand
or kept their petals closed tightly
as mouths exhausted of language.

The author knew that to name flowers
would give us pictures of the ones we know.
The ones that have been stepped on or torn away.
And so they become the idea of flowers,
aligned in straight rows,
colours bright as television garb.

The man and woman photogenic,
no lines in their faces.
We do not see their hair when they awaken,
have no awkward images of their first time.
Without parents or movies,
would they know how the parts fit?

It has become an old favourite,
the story that ends without bickering or boredom,
forced apart by fate,
an act of God.

How often we use the term now: falling out
of something we have made
in the absence of description.

If only our story ended the same:
with a bang not a whimper.
If only we followed their example
and did not stay long enough
to see the seasons change.

THAT NIGHT

We decorate the past with gin martinis,
that night, now, heavy as an olive pit
sinking in your coffee mug.
If we drink and talk long and fast
enough, the past will bend like a pine branch
beneath cotton snow, and

I won't go home with her, after all.
We are past that now,
quickly approaching the beginning,
the invisible rip in your summer dress
and smile, that night,
now, clear as vermouth.

HAROLD AND MAUDE

There's you with a crown of dandelions,
legs crossed, our knees touching.
I watch your eyes move in small circles
to imitate the seasons as you play guitar.

There's me singing along
as you play Cat Stevens.
There's you laughing at me,
because I don't know the words.
Each time I want to give up
you call me Harold
and start the song again.

You are too young to be Maude,
but just as kind.

There's us in a movie
about two people falling in love,
soundtrack written and performed by Cat Stevens.

This is my favourite memory of us.
Even though you would never wear flowers in your hair,
can't play guitar
and hate Cat Stevens,
the rest is more or less true.

I'M NOT HERE FOR SUSHI

Monday, 10 p.m. I hang up the phone, hard.
Put on the nearest pair of pants: the ones on the floor.
I do not check them for stains or cat hair,
which I know must be there. The T-shirt I find draped over the TV
has the name of a band on it I haven't listened to in five years.
I walk to the sushi restaurant on the next block:
the closest place to get a drink.
On the patio I watch the dead sun of a streetlamp
break apart in the harbour.
At the tables across: two couples,
large ceramic plates spread before them,
their sushi set out in symmetrical rows
and, I suspect, colour coordinated.

A compliment or flirtation, something resembling a promise
wafts over from the tables.
I try and fail to collect their words into a story:
an aesthetically pleasing arrangement of raw fish.
I no longer know what it is a man and woman speak about
over dinner, only that there is a law
about loving or hating fully;
there is the rule about having a pleasant evening.
My beer arrives and I focus my attention
on more important things
like watching ash break away from my cigarette.
The couples are watching, I think. Wish that I would drink alone
on a bar stool in some place with muted televisions
and half price chicken wings.
They went out to be "out"
and talk of nothing in particular,
not to see this.

But I'm here, I think,
just like the coffee stain on my pants.
The party cruise boats dock along the harbour,
neon lights along their sides, people with Hawaiian shirts,
red and blue drinks in their hands,
slices of fruit on the glass rims.
And the piña colada song.

I can deal with
the cancers and betrayals, the wars and suicides,
even the way everything has its fine point,
where the next movement, even a breath,
will snap it in half.
How love is no different, perhaps, faith too.
But that fucking piña colada song is the last straw.

I get the bill, put the little green mint in my mouth
and suck on it.

A JOKE
(for Golnaz)

Forgive me.

I never said it was funny.

Any of it.

LAST THROES

Darling, there is a space between your shoulder blades, so small,
I am certain no other mouth has ever been there.
The others (since we've been apart,
how many have there been?)
were careless, letting lust interfere with exploration.
I should give that space a name
and plant a flag.
This is love: imperialism
with nothing to gain.

It doesn't matter anymore
why we're here. We're at love
and need to choose sides.
It's too late, now, to say things like I'm sorry
I never wrote you an apology poem,
now that I would only apologize
or refuse to as an entrance strategy.

Perhaps, this time you will greet me as a liberator.

WINTER (AN APOLOGY)

Here we are, crossing this once-white page,
now the colour of exhaust

and time sped up, ground to pulp
under hurried steps.

Winter moves slowly,
it seems —

we have failed again
to make Spring arrive like an apology,

despite our most sacred rituals.

We barely resemble the effigies
we have made of each other. Burning,

more to keep us warm
than to appease any particular god.

It would be difficult for a pagan,
never mind a communist,

                    to love you
                    according to the season,

to know, finally, how to decorate an altar
is more important (sometimes) than believing in it.

I guess, this is your apology poem, after all.

                        Sorry

it doesn't ask forgiveness
for a single thing I did.

Sorry it took me so long
to understand an apology
like winter is mostly
a description of absence.

APOLLO

You cannot follow a woman to the riverbank
anymore. There is always a bridge
or restraining order.

STUFF

I'm not a Buddhist,
I just hate stuff.
It's different from detachment —
I am very attached to my hatred of things.

I am taking a stand,
maybe even declaring war
on dining sets and colour coordination.

There is no collateral damage in the war on silverware
and matching socks.
The battle is fought with passive resistance
(I am kind of like Gandhi in this way).

My black and grey socks are concealed beneath my pant legs,
and you don't get much of a reaction when you sneer
at stuff in the windows along Yorkville.

But I'm winning.
Nothing matches in my room.
It is the green zone
in the war on stuff.

Sometimes I wish I had a lot of money
to buy art and women under the guise of love.
The women not the art that is.
Art is Buddhist or feline; it asks nothing from you,
except that you pay attention.
But don't get me started on love.
That's in section 4.6 of the manifesto.

We should burn all our possessions,
the world would be more spacious.
I would burn all my possessions now, truly I would,
But isn't fire just another thing?
Isn't a poem?

No, art is not stuff.
Because you can never own Ophelia
or expect Girl with a Mandolin
to make you feel secure.

4.6:
You can buy into love
and never own it.
Love is a flat pyramid scheme.
It is neither stuff nor art
but it is something,
though I am against things I don't understand.
But I don't hate them –
god and love.
I've heard they are the same thing.
This is so absurd, it might be true.
I respect that
as much as I hate
that love requires an equal amount of respect and loathing.
Why am I having trouble getting laid recently?

To review:
stuff bad, art good.

Love, be it resolved . . .
Can't you see that every manifesto from Marx to Breton is
asking a very simple question.

Why don't you love me (enough)?

MY RELIGIOUS UPBRINGING

In my mother's home
we had a Christmas tree
and a menorah.
All my friends had trees in their homes,
so, naturally, I wanted one as well.
My mother, not wanting me to feel too different
or too Jewish, agreed.
It was a fair compromise:
we were Jewish,
but not excessively Jewish.
We were just the right amount of Jewish.

In my father's home
there wasn't a tree
or a menorah.
"Why can't we have a Christmas tree
or at least a candle tree?" I pleaded.
He looked down at me, paused for effect,
and in his most serious voice,
which was very, very serious, said:
"Religion is the opiate of the masses."
This was not open to compromise.

In my mother's home
there was also a statue of Buddha,
but this was purely for decoration.

THE LANGUAGE OF OUR PEOPLE

She held the book like an infant,
tightly, so the yellow and worn pages would not slip away,
but gently, lest they be torn from their spine.
She read aloud from it, to it, whispering
what she called the language of our people.

When she died, the book became an orphan,
babeling a story, familiar
yet confounded by language,
los t/s and distan t/ce.

At her funeral, the rabbi spoke
in English and the language of our people.
He didn't know she died before *Exodus*
(and would have barely understood a word),
that something was,
is, always,
lost in translation.

WHEN THE REVOLUTION COMES

I will be right behind you,
stones in hand, though they're heavy
and you, Papa, are a giant,
tall enough for one to stop
at the back of your head.

FOOTAGE FROM HAIFA

Rockets are falling near my father's home
or inside it, him
now rubble, for all I know.
We have not spoken since I made my demands:
for everything he has taken
or not given.
I won't confirm or deny any responsibility
for the rockets,
but I sympathize with the militants,

envy the dislocated victims
of televised wars.
The attention they receive,
carrying the remains of lives
on their backs
through a homeland, disfigured, unrecognizable.
How they get to feel
the pain of the other side,
expressed without ambivalence.

RED DIASPORA

I.

Traced back, close to St. Mark's Church,
East Village, above a laundry mat, a small tribe
born of absences, God, wealth, culture
begins in London and, or St. Petersburg. We won't argue
if the true origin is theory
or practice, at least not for too long.
We agreed it was worth dying for,
killing too –
piety indistinguishable from mourning
for the Zion we never had, or perhaps for a short time,
between McCarthy and Perestroika, between
Houston and Bleecker. The ghetto built with a fallen wall,
the ghetto built in the souls we do not have;
what happens when one has faith
only in humanity. My father lost in his long coat,
buying a loaf of rye and Campbell's chicken soup, for one.
He has arrived. Another white face in Toronto,
treated like everyone else, no star on his sleeve
or hammer and sickle, only a little dirt and dried snot.
Though he knows it would make no difference,
condemned not to silence,
but discounts and *TV Guide*.

II.

We have not moved
far from home, only east.
I make the pilgrimage
from water's edge to Cabbagetown and you,
a little further, Jewish Quarter,
Scarborough, Dawes Road Cemetery,
among your people.

Home used to be plump with Brooklyn
accent, Jewish when angry or tired
of Marx and Steinem, eyes
heavy with 'ists spreading
like the disease driving you out
of your body, longing to be another
Ashkenazi mother and wife, afraid
of God instead of Reagan.

Though Bukovina wasn't your home,
was New York? Toronto? Marxist Utopia
that never was. Home
is the places you didn't belong
inside of you, growing
as tumors, decaying soon like remnants
of uprooted settlements, Berlin Wall,
Alphabet City, mine,
yours, the father's looks
and ideals, rotting.

III.

Force fed promises,
intravenous milk and honey, morphine.
Identity defined by who she thought I was
in the last visiting hour.

It was either Israel or pills.
I had to choose forgiveness,
finding my father
decorated in chipped paint
and black scorpions: medals
of poverty; apartment in Maoist aesthetic,
overlooking the Holy Sepulchre,

our north star to the synagogue.
"We make a left at the big cross," you said,
and "I will wear the yarmulke,
but not pray." Hoping, perhaps,
this would make up for missing the funeral.

Your finger guiding my eyes
through the Hebrew text.
You seemed embarrassed because I stuttered
over the Kaddish,
or were you just ashamed
that I was seeking peace,
instead of change.

After, I told you I felt nothing;
you seemed satisfied
as if you had taught me something.

I am not sure, still,
what I asked of God,
though the answer finds me now, Toronto:
your streets familiar as her palms.
Yet I become lost
from your memory, so quickly
and never fast enough.

II

here,

poetry can't hurt you

East Village seven dollars and one drink minimum, August 19,
    2006. The still living, lucid minds of Ginsberg's generation
    talking *Howl* and "America" in a café on the cleaned up,
    gentrified bottom of the rivers of Bowery.
Amiri Baraka saying, "You gotta polish words like guns,
    sharpen'em like knives to slice open the social fabric, reveal
    it starving, hysterical naked. That's how *Howl* changed
    America," he says while polishing off an Amstel, while his
    face and fiery speech, and the words Bowery   Poetry   Club
    clothed in shadow, while that beer's lit up in the centre of
    the stage like a product placement shot in some Hollywood
    retrospective on Beatnik culture.
Now, old hipsters and hippies turned academics take their turn,
    like Gordon Ball comparing *Howl* to *The Waste Land*, or
    Alicia Ostriker paralleling the poem to Old Testament
    scripture, lecture entitled "Is *Howl* Jewish? Are 'the Best
    Minds' Yids?"
But, I fear the best minds are no longer, the best minds were the
    ones destroyed by madness, or the ones who grew up and
    got real jobs. And maybe *Howl* did change America, but into
    what?
Or were we all too busy stroking each other's cocks, and patting
    each other on the backs and asses – letting ourselves be
    fucked by saintly motorcyclists, screaming with joy,
    celebrating our victory over pure machinery and running
    money – to notice America was changing back, that Moloch
    was growing bigger, hungrier, adapting, mutating, winding his
    way through the bushes and hairy assholes of our literary
    Edens? Is this the inevitable result of what happens when
    everybody's holy, when everyman's an angel?
But isn't this fashionable nihilism what Moloch gorges on? Wake
    up, man. This is what it's all about; real Beat era poets

reminiscing in The East Village. Amiri Baraka sending you
out into the streets of New York, armed to the teeth, or at
least balls, with words, saying, "Go fuck yourself with your
atom bomb . . . now that's poetry. You see a poet's gotta
make language cut fine, precise wounds into the heart of
culture, cause that's the gig. It ain't easy, but that's the gig
and you can't wait for it, read your poems in the streets,
paste 'em to signposts if you have to!"

Yeah, that's it – fuck this pathetic whining for approval, fuck this
pandering to some whitewashed academic publishing
aesthetic, trying to get in some journal people only read for
submission guidelines.

It's about the words, it's about having something to say, words as
weapons just like Baraka with that Amstel in his hand,
dripping with condensation, glittering as if on a Times Square
billboard, illuminated like angels staggering on tenement
roofs; the tenements that have been torn down and turned to
condos and Starbucks.

Though I could use a latté, before I get started, before I deliver
the first blow to CanLit sensibility. No, I need a drink. I need
to get drunk and go stumbling through the stale beer
afternoon, float across the tops of cities contemplating . . .

Fuck, I'm not contemporary enough for publication. I'm too
narrative, too personal. Or, I should just tell CanLit to "go
fuck yourself with your regional aesthetics." But that's not
subversive enough on a syntactic level. Dissent is a subtle
reworking of language, which is most successful when it goes
unnoticed, according to my last rejection letter. I need to be
more image driven, no, language driven, no, sound driven. I
need to read more Greek and Roman mythology, so I can
reference it. I need a drink.

An ice cold Amstel would really hit the spot right now.

BREAKFAST POEM
(for Frank O'Hara)

we have never spoken on the telephone
or been alive at the same time
though sometimes I am not winning
sometimes I am quite not alive
sitting here with my gigantic mug of coffee
and an open window and a blank screen
          you should see this mug Frank I can get half my face in it
but the coffee gets cold too quickly and nothing happens
on the page
where are you
in all this white hysteria
buying newspapers (I've never heard of) and crèpes perhaps
from a vendor in Central Park somewhere

it is not just me I think
trying to navigate the snow-covered paths of the Ramble
in Toronto in my bedroom
you should see my room Frank
there simply isn't space
for words or lovers
I can't even find my socks
          did you know I have beautiful lips?
they are round and full like an Italian movie star
but the rest of me
is not so silver
I mean there doesn't seem to be much of a point
in writing or wearing a long coat
or thinking about Manhattan
since Fire Island

I don't like strange accidents
like poems the world is too messy
you should see this planet Frank
I can't find my keys amongst all this jazz and newsprint skylines
          and what about hands? They're so useful and leaf-like
I guess it's not such a bad place really
really when it snows and people must choose
between warmth and style
these days I am donning something thick but not puffy
          I can't picture you Frank O'Hara wearing anything
but a long grey coat or something with a collar
smoking on St. Mark's Place
which just hasn't been the same since I've been alive
besides you shouldn't smoke too many cigarettes
and love so much
it's bad for you
but so are beach buggies I've heard

ALEXANDRIA

In a café bar, my generation drinks and talks
of going places, though where, exactly, no one seems to know.
Beautiful, important places –
lily painted vases or something. I wasn't paying attention,
lost in a poor imitation of Durrell's *Quartet*.
The dusty patio lamps of this café bringing me back to the nights
I drank and walked alone down the narrow streets of Alexandria
with Justine
nowhere to be found.
And the dusty lamps illuminated
the thin neck of a warm bottle.

The beer is colder here, though more expensive –
this conversation about all the important things I'm doing,
bringing me closer to something . . . But I'm tired.
Tired of trying to pass knowledge off as wisdom like Salinger said.
And worse, trying to transform the wisdom of others
into my own.

Maybe, I shouldn't be here at all,
but at home studying structural functionalism,
so I can be a journalist.
I don't want to always end up at café bars,
talking about what I want to do with my life.
I'd rather just be doing it.

Did Charles Bukowski aspire to *be* something
or did he just write?
Bukowski was an old man when the bender finally survived him.
He must have been hoping to die on a bar stool
like Dylan Thomas or shot like Lorca.

Is this not the ultimate ambition:
a life worthy of a bullet?
He must have been just waiting for that glorious day
when the back of his skull would shatter and illuminate
like Haydn and cold beer at 4:30 a.m.
But people were too busy reading the newspaper
to know words meant something.
It didn't take them long in Spain,
but here, here, poetry can't hurt you.

I was watching one of those shows
where mothers bring their daughters on TV
to tell them what bad people they've become.
It wasn't Springer –
the mothers didn't hit their girls with chairs,
just called them sluts.

And I can't remember what was wrong with the daughters.
They were too fat or on drugs or both.
And I started thinking, if my daughter was too fat or on drugs,
I'd still be happy I had a daughter.
I'd still be proud of her
for being alive.

And then I thought, if I ever have kids,
I'll be nice to them in the first place
so they won't get too fat or do drugs,
at least not a lot of drugs.
And I won't let them watch Springer,
maybe not even the news.
And I won't die
before they're twenty-five,
maybe thirty.

You can't go on Springer by yourself.
It's just not entertaining.

I've been thinking about moving to Tibet
and becoming a Buddhist,
but I don't know what to pack.

Which reminds me,
I don't think conditioner does anything,
but I'm afraid not to use it,
just in case.

The problem with all those pictures of Jesus
is they never show him with carpenters' hands.
He always has clean, smooth fingers.
It's just not believable.

There's this vegetarian restaurant in Prague,
owned by Hare Krishnas. They seemed nice
and the food was cheap,
but after a while they started to recognize me
and smiled and said "Hare Krishna."
And I'd say "Hare Krishna" back to them,
because I didn't want to be rude.
I didn't want to tell them
I like my hair and turtlenecks too much
to ever be one of them.
But then again,
I guess I wouldn't "need" conditioner.

Jesus didn't use it
and he turned out okay.

I think I like Jesus,
but I don't love him.
He seems like an alright guy,
someone to walk with in Yorkville,
pretending to have money.

But they can always tell —
even if I was with Jesus,
they would still think they're better than me.

That's okay. It's how evolution works:
I'm better than the people on Springer
and the people in Yorkville are better than me.

I can accept this
and I can accept Jesus
with manicured hands
and the mothers
who would rather be famous for a day
than kind.

DEAR OFFICE OF HOMELAND SECURITY

It's my duty to inform you I saw a flag waving suspiciously
outside Grand Central Station.

I held my hands to my ears and opened my mouth
and stood on one leg,
trying to signal the authorities
just like the website told me to,
but was only given quarters by a street mime.

So I bought beer nuts from a guy standing next to a guy selling
watches, because you can't buy sugar coated nuts on the streets
in Canada and I wanted to know what it meant to be an American.

And the flag moved so smugly,
not selling or buying anything,
just standing there with a golden rod
protruding from its rear,
displayed proudly as peacock feathers.

No one seemed to notice how the flag's stripes were expanding,
spreading across the city, towards the ocean.

I began to run across 42nd Street,
a trail of beer nuts behind me,
making my way to Times Square,
because I thought I should see *The Lion King*
or smoke crack
before I die,
but could afford neither.
There, I hid amongst the plush animals of the Disney Store
and by a gigantic Mickey Mouse head I sat down and wept.

BLAZON FOR A STRANGER

I want you to know
I am not angry or disappointed in you
for falling on me when the train stopped.
You may have overestimated the tightness
of your grip around the pole
or your ability to find the centre of gravity.
These things happen.
And I know the person
in train stations and cafés,
eating lunch or scratching the inside of their ear,
is only your disguise.
No one knows the real you:
the hero who keeps cities from sinking into oceans
and giants from crushing our sun.
You do this every night, alone in your room,
taking no credit,
like the day you narrowed the width of all the tornadoes.
No one but you remembers that they were once the size of Tokyo,
ripping entire forests from the earth,
tearing trees off like band-aids.
And each time a handful of people are torn apart in these winds,
you are relieved,
for you know they once killed the dinosaurs.

And now you are holding your travel mug with the faulty lid,
coffee staining your shirt,
while standing next to you is a woman reeking of whiskey
and stories no one will listen to.

But I know who you are
when you step on my foot.
You always thought it was just you and the vampires
who lived forever.
You don't recognize me without the Victorian beard
or green scales.
I stood next to you when we stormed the Bastille
and when the king's severed head came rolling from the guillotine
we nearly kissed amongst the cheering crowds
like it was New Year's Eve.

METHOD SUICIDE

When Konstantin kills himself,
the actor is off-stage not even pretending to kill himself.
This is why Chekhov was so brilliant and died
only three years after falling in love for the first time. Of course,
Chekhov was saying something about plot
having little to do with events. If *The Seagull* were fiction,
Constantine's brain splatter
would fall neatly between a set of brackets.

The phone rang like a gunshot
in the other room. I nearly believed you that time,
though you were playing too many characters
for a realist comedy. You cannot be Konstantin
and at the same time tell Trigorin/the audience,
"You have just killed yourself!"
The whole thing felt a little Brechtian:
your near death stimulating
only on an intellectual level –
suicide as social gest.

This is why you will never be a great actress.
You can't just want to die.
You have to live it.
This is what separates the great performances from the mediocre
(I think my mother trained with Stanislavsky).

Chekhov frequented brothels.
He was incapable of trusting or loving a woman,
which might not be different things.

I didn't leave you after the first attempt,
only because I was reading *Lady with Lapdog* at the time
and I thought Chekhov was saying that suffering was a requisite
for authentic love.
I didn't know he was just telling a story,
that suffering is just a description of the landscape,
that love is the only requisite for love.

WOMEN

All the women I tried to save
have survived my attempts at rescuing.
They are with other men or God
or themselves. Either way
someone more suitable.
And despite and maybe even because
of the betrayals, the theft of many things,
I wish them well on their treks
over flour heaps and steeples,
over hills made of sheets, pillows and other
sharp objects. Some have taught me
to inhale moonlight and find angels
in Chinatown dumpsters,
allow candy wrappers and rotted fruit
their proper cling and pull.
Yes, I suppose women taught me
through my tutorials,
lectures really, on authenticity
and responsibility, on living
in texts. But I won't
claim we're any better for it,
just a little more beautiful
now that we will never see each other
naked again.

FEAR AND TREMBLING
(REGINE OLSEN'S LAMENT)

"Is there a teleological suspension of the ethical?"

— Søren Kierkegaard

Your hunch was somehow smooth
the year we were in love.
And the rumour about your penis
must have been a lie.
It would not have been curved, but direct
as a prayer inside me —
you are not a man of letters.
But a myth: the merman, torn
between his desire to marry Agnes
and duty to save her
through abandonment.

Now only my version remains:
the merman who does not try to rise from the depths
but to them, who is unafraid
to let Agnes truly get her feet wet; faith
you could have been loved
by and through your deformities:
bent seductions, back misshapen
by heavy concepts.
If only you could have suspended your need
to always move towards a purpose,
understood love outside a text.

Regine Olsen was engaged to Søren Kierkegaard from September 1840 until
October 1841. Kierkegaard unexpectedly broke off the engagement.

YOUR HAUNTED HOUSE

There were so many empty rooms in your uncle's house,
we never could have stayed together long enough
to make love in all of them.
I sometimes wonder if I invented that place
with its five washrooms, with its Jacuzzi and wood paneled sauna
that no one used. The billiards room with its flawless pool table;
the green felt that looked like the always freshly mowed yard.
Sometimes, when everyone was at work or in distant rooms
I would play pool by myself
and listen to the balls knock against each other:
the only noise in that gigantic quiet.
It sounded like ghosts meeting each other in haunted corridors,
even when everyone was home
in their separate rooms.

Your uncle was loud, angry
and rarely seen.
You told me never to talk to him.
I don't know if he was different before his wife died.
He seemed like the kind of man who is born with a dead spouse,
who only knows how to accumulate wealth and tragedy.
You told me your mother barely spoke as well
before she sent you to live there.
And how many times were you silent
while throwing dishes at me. Did no one else hear them
smashing against the bedroom wall?
Were the rooms, really, so far apart?
I imagine that days went by in that house,
with no one saying a word
as if you were all preparing to become ghosts,
and this was the only thing you had to look forward to.

It is nearly ten years now, since we made love,
quietly, between those walls.
Occasionally, you send me a letter
from your new home with your husband in Australia –
as far away from that house as possible.
You send me photographs: you in your long, extravagant dress
and smile.
And I don't feel jealous
or happy for you. You are not the same girl who lived among ghosts,
just another woman in a white dress. But, I'm glad
I can remember the splintered wine glasses,
the thud of pool balls breaking a thick silence,
that cold and quiet sauna,
footsteps like bones cracking;
the sounds of perpetual departing – the only evidence now
of how much I must have been in love with you.

TWENTY MINUTES AWAY IN ANOTHER CONTINENT

They've been demolishing that bank all summer.
Sledgehammers against brick and glass. And still,
I can hear you
making love to him.

(I live in Europe. You're in Asia,
and I can almost see your house.)

They take the walls down from the inside,
as if from a nest,
borrowed under skin.

(When you walk down to the harbour,
to observe the light of a hundred mosques,
do you try to see my house?)

Windows smashed in like the teeth
of a corrupt (but *honest*) official, body floating
like a gaze across the Bosphorus.

(We are divided by water.)

ISTANBUL

I love you? Are you love me?
Well, at least he wasn't using you
for your teaching skills.
Nothing in the contract about fucking your students.
Since there was no contract.
> *Always keep at least 50 million lire*
> *for bribes.*
American currency and blue eyes help too.

I could have murdered you
and gotten away with it.

LOVE POEM

It's perfectly fine that you've gone back to him,
the promiscuous kick-boxer
who fucked two prostitutes
while you were out buying cabbage
(for his soup). Truth be told, I don't know
if you ever make soup,
but if you do, I'm certain it isn't too salty –
and I have never slept with a hooker or kicked anyone
in the face.

It's probably for the best. I don't have time to pursue you
all the way to the river bank
or even the concrete slab bordering the campus pond.
I'm much too busy developing my poetics
and not being a john.
I just don't have the time to effortlessly undo your gown
of bark and laurels, to uproot your heart
from that cold earth.

Besides, nothing can compete with the romance
we are having here.
How our bodies form constellations.
How we spend the afternoons, arrayed in flannel,
sipping your just salty enough cabbage soup.
How your (ex)boyfriend accepts fate
and doesn't beat me senseless.
How our passion only grows more luminous
like an always waxing moon.
How your love in that imagined and oh so real life
will surpass and shame this idea of it.

REALISM AND ANTI-REALISM

You can't close the eyelids of the recently dead.
They spring right back like broken venetian blinds.

*Many philosophers prefer simple ontologies populated with only the bare
minimum of types of entities.*

Last night, I received this email from my philosophy professor:
"I apologize for canceling classes,
but my father had a heart attack . . ."

*A statement is meaningful if and only if it is either analytically or
empirically verifiable.*

"I administered CPR,
but it was too late."

At night, the Western Desert looks like the surface of the moon.

"I know you all understand and I don't want to talk about it,

                    teaching my classes will get me through this."

I want to tell you
                    Any entity that isn't observed

Sometimes my mother comes back, worm eaten, decayed and

                    is one we are not forced to admit.

I am embarrassed to be seen with her.

An overpopulated universe is in many ways unlovely . . .

In Farafra, I took all my clothes off and floated
in a desert hot spring.

It offends the aesthetic sense of us who have a taste for desert scapes.

There were more stars in the sky than empty space.

KADDISH FOR ARIEL SHARON

You are now just another disputed border
between the homes of the living and the dead.
An imperialist, even now, relentless, terminal.

Mourning or celebration seems too easy
for the passing of any man.
Even though I suspect
you were born with only the idea of a heart,
something pumps blood to your body,
as you sleep through the demolitions and air strikes.

Somewhere your children avoid buses
and cry sea salt, as you cannot even raise your hand to bless them.
And though it sounds a little distorted,
like corked wind chimes, the bell tolls for you too.
A piece of the continent, a part of the main,
regardless of who it belongs to, will soon wash away.

WHAT KEEPS ME UP AT NIGHT

I am afraid.
Afraid that art and love
are merely hobbies
and should only be consummated
on 15 minute coffee breaks –
or they are only the ornaments,
the holiday décor
of shopping malls.

I am afraid
that Bukowski was wrong.
What matters most is not how well you walk through the fire,
but how well you walk around it
or find a way to sell it
to the wealthy and the bored.

I am afraid.
Afraid I don't understand "the markets,"
any of them.
And this is the only fire left
people are willing
to walk through.

I am afraid
books are more commodity
than prayer.

And I have the same fear
for prayers.

III

can it ever be

cancelled?

NOVEMBER ELEGY

> ". . . having been once, though only once,
> having been once on earth — can it ever be cancelled?"
>
> — Rilke

Sky dense with migration.
Seagulls escaping the winter
like warmth from your body.
Shriveled and luminous
yellow leaves, hands, still open
against the November current.
Your lung collapsing like a promise
or phone ringing in the night.
All these wires crossing the Atlantic,
carrying Chris's voice
over the Charles Bridge
and Castle steps. Breaking apart
with static, hesitation. The unexpected news
I had been waiting for, suddenly, all my life. I didn't know,
      I didn't know Rilke was born into this city then.
Somehow, I think this would have mattered,
without making the slightest difference.
If only I had looked at the sky, I could have been with you
in Toronto or New York City, June 6, 1968,
as you scrawled on the inside cover
of your beaten and yellowed Elegies
in my hands only now, five years after
and yet, always, it seems, sharing this text.
The lines in your palm underlining *neither childhood nor future*
are growing less . . . Supernumerous existence
wells up in my heart more as the years increase in number,
as the past moves further away like roots grown long enough,
now, only now, to finally wrap around each other.

TRICKING INTO SUICIDE
(for Chris)

Summer ends out here,
this canoe floor stained with beer and cigarettes,
paddles cutting the still water, silver, mercury.
Styx or the last river
after the sun has burnt out.
We are conquering empires,
the maples burning red or orange
like the fires of Troy.
We are men at the edge of history.
We are anything we want to be
for this last hour of sunlight, of summer —

ending out here with you,
the kid who smoked me my first joint
and told me my mother was dying.
Now, teaching me how to trick fish into suicide.
You roll your eyes when I put it this way,
frustrated that I've never learned to live fully
in any one moment.
Maybe, like how to make a bong from a pop bottle,
one day, you'll teach me that too.

The worm wriggles between my fingers and craps on my palm.
You laugh, then shrug, pretending you weren't expecting it.
And I know this too is some kind of lesson.
Something about how even shit in your hand
can be a gift.

We are silent now, so as not to scare the fish out of dying.
And there is time, or nothing else to do
but look closely at your face, notice

how I have not noticed you age.
How twenty years appear
in the length of time it takes to cast and reel back
an empty hook.
The way age comes on like autumn,
overnight, leaves stained orange and red,
and you wake to find the summer thickness fallen from the air.

The way the words *engagement* and *career*
have wriggled from the mouths of more and more of our friends.
How there are only so many years left before we say these things too
or feel like failures because we don't.
A tug on my line and you show me
how to reel it in, gently.
And after I pull its body, no larger than my hand,
out of the water, I wonder if, after this,
there will be anything left to learn for the first time.

I am relieved when you say that I should throw it back.
You tell me to squeeze its gills in my fist
and I nearly rip the head off.
My eyes fix on the fish guts dangling from the hook.
You tell me not to worry, that it will forget about it in four seconds
and I can't help but feel envious –
its memory too short for anything to ever really end.

COLLECTING

It happens in pieces.
Begins with unfurled sails,
white boats, still, between the ice sheets,
the shut mouth of a mailbox.

Isn't this what people do, walk places, look at things,
bend down to tie a shoelace, shield eyes from the sun,
and somewhere in there feel something?

It has something to do with a man
walking his dog in February,
hands wrapped in plastic, the secret
still steaming from the snow.

And you know a part of it as well,
knitting in the bus shelter.
Although it will be gone, once you notice
my face through the glass.

Is it the thing you are feeling now
as you touch the ends of needles together
or now, as you draw them apart?

You cannot say
what happens in between
notes, as wrinkled palms
compress the fat spine
of an accordion on a subway platform.

Another train stops,
pulls away.
It will be the next one
or the one after that.

GHOSTS

They can walk and talk just like real people.
They begin to vanish first from the inside,
not because they're shot or stabbed
or because of a disease, but because
something has caused them to forget —
and if they could remember
the thing they are forgetting,
they would tell you.
They would not be
becoming ghosts.

GOD

"Canst thou draw out leviathan
with an hook? Or his tongue
with a cord which thou lettest down?"

— Job: 41:1

No, but I beat Leviathan
to ashes and lily pollen.

How?

With love, my Lord,
I defeated You with love.

CHRISTMAS

He's come back like every year
turning over the tables
of free samples in the shopping malls,
watching by the water fountain,
everything given over to some Caesar or another.
He tries not to judge or preach,
just whispers to the young woman
parking her stroller, letting fall
several bags weighing like eyelids
and taking in
the cool waters,
something about love, forgiveness . . .
He is cut off
by mall security
at the request of the good customers,
who are just trying to spend and beat
traffic. He doesn't struggle. He doesn't respond
to requests for identity.
He walks out in grace
and humiliation.
And I am tempted to follow,
but I'm with close friends
and afraid they'll abandon me.
So he hops the Queen turnstile,
heads north, then east,
grasping the metal pole
to keep steady, waiting
for the end of the line.

D I

Tossed from the horse drawn wagons
and the cross, beaten like Jacob
without blessing, for parting
the cracked lips
of oral narratives.

They were so relentless, I know, I know
with their stones, breaking glass houses, bodies.
And how much longer did the bruises stay
when made from attempts to love —

throwing it into the sea
as a child skips a stone,
knowing it won't come back,
least not in the same form.
But oh, how it ripples,
how it ripples, Di.

PACHELBEL'S CANON

If poured through the speakers instead of Wagner,
history would not alter. The same lines
and grave markers of Eastern Europe
would still be in my palm –
releasing dry skin like feathers
migrating to warmer seasons
or windshields,
as the Canon lullabies into the afternoon.
Through the tree line, the soft, splintered light
is the same on my shoulders
as my face since the song began.
Little has changed, only the tint of sky, a strand of hair
shifted out of place. Nothing really changes
in music, it's just rearranged. And still
it's the only rational justification, right now,
for this being alive, this Sunday stroll out of history.
Somewhere, Heaven is ashamed,
every time these paper symbols are translated to sound,
translated to nothing
I can find fault with.
And there goes the telephone cord and electric light
and as much as possible, my lungs and heart.
Listening to the deceased ascending,
and you and I and the twentieth century are forgiven,
for the length of a violin string.

GHOST STORY

There is only the love of ghosts with me tonight
and it would be cruel
to suggest someone in this room doesn't know
how to love, or exist for that matter.
We know how to love perfectly well, they would say,
if they had voices
that could be heard by living ears, or thought
anything worthwhile ever happened by the word.
We know how to love, they say,
with the distant steps of horses
with the strength of the north wind
rattling the thick glass
around a memory.
We love with an ancient desire
that cannot contain a woman
or world. We love according to eternal laws
that have as much substance, here,
as a winter breath or promise
to love more fully,
this time. We know how to love
on moonless nights
when the telephone is still life
and shadows knock against you
like ghosts
who can only love this much.

UNTITLED

I hope there is a God
he doesn't have to do
or say

                         anything

just exist
and not judge me
like a good poem

and I wish I still had

                   a mother

she doesn't have to do

                 more than God

maybe just tell me
I am kind
even if she's only saying it
because she is my mother

and I would like there to be

                a woman

next to me
naked and smoking
a cigarette
she doesn't have to do
anything either
only tell me I am good
and that it's alright
if there is no God
and there are no mothers

I just might believe her
and sleep for awhile

IN HER VOICE

I see, you know
though not in the way you think of seeing.
I am not a ghost.
The dead don't care
for that term.
It's like when someone calls your poem a piece,
or wish, a prayer.
It's not kosher, as we used to say.

I can't watch all the time,
the life of the spirit is full.
Yes, the dead are busy
at work, at grace.
I could try to explain it to you
but there is an old saying here,
roughly translated:
one who gains through knowledge will leave
with everything but wisdom.
Although that's not quite right, only

close to paradise
is anything
but perfect.
It's allowing, embracing
pure foolishness.

I know I was a better poet
while alive, that I had a talent for detail,
but here it is a failing
or rather impossibility,
like translating wind chimes,
like what I am doing right now.

Yesterday, I saw you enter
the house for the blind.
Last time you were there
you tried to pretend it was a dream,
but could not ignore the evidence:
your flooded eyes.

Since you have stopped wishing
and learned to pray
(though you have much to learn about prayer),
I have begun to watch
more carefully, although not in this order
or any for that matter.
This is why, sometimes, you think
you can hear my breath
like a rain so light,
you are unsure if it is falling
or about to.

I know at night you read Rilke
and think of me
and you read what you hear:
the good singing.

And as you sat in Astoria, speaking to Di,
watching the flare and distortion of the overhead lights,
burning only for you,
saying how you felt silly,
but seeing better was, of course, more important,
did you hear yourself?

You never sang so well.

CHOICE

You liked candles and stars,
anything that glowed
and eventually burned out.
You liked the ocean
and fucking, bodies you did not discriminate,
loved for being what they led to,
even a shattered home
on the beaches of Fire Island –
walking there amongst the skeletal frames,
the shape of abandonment
you loved
everything that sought to awe
as much as destroy.

You liked spiders, wooden pipes, bourbon on the rocks
and valium.
Standard conversation at the dinner table:
movies, the weather (storms)
and rape. Maybe you liked how a face contorted at the word,
while shoveling mash potatoes into its mouth
or just didn't care. You had the floor
and no one had the balls
to take it away from you,
because you were sick
of things, of taken:

childhood, the right to choose
and later your left, then right breast.
How you had to consent to another rape
to maybe live.
No guarantees, the men told you,
this is the best we've got:

chop and slice
nearly your wrists, though more moderate now –
opposed to violence,
you swallowed a bottle of pills,
put on *Law and Order*
and went to sleep.

Woke up in the hospital bed,
screaming at me
for calling the ambulance:
asshole, bastard, how dare I –
become this kind of man,
blaming the victim, and worse,
thinking it was my right to choose
how you should not die.